God's
Name
Is Love

Daily Reflections of
CARLO CARRETTO

Foreword by Morton Kelsey

God's Name Is Love

edited and introduced
by
Fr. Joseph Diele

New City Press

Published in the United States by New City Press
202 Cardinal Rd., Hyde Park, NY 12538
©1996 New City Press

Illustrations by Duncan Harper
Cover design by Nick Cianfarani

Library of Congress Cataloging-in-Publication Data:

Carretto, Carlo.
    God's name is love : daily reflections of Carlo Carretto / edited
and introduced by Joseph Diele ; foreword by Morton Kelsey.
        p.   cm.
    ISBN 1-56548-079-1 (pbk.)
    1. Spiritual life—Catholic Church.   2. Meditations.   I. Diele,
Joseph.   II. Title.
BX2182.2.C33   1996
242—dc20   96-28010

2d printing: December 2000

Printed in the United States of America

Contents

Foreword

Few books have touched me as deeply as these words of Little Brother Carlo Carretto. I have been on a serious religious journey for over fifty years. These healing and inspired reflections have resonated and confirmed my own deepest spiritual experience. They have fed my soul. Usually I groan when I am asked to write a foreword for an author I have not known well. However, this time I have become more and more grateful that I was asked to write a foreword to this magnificent collection of passages from fourteen of the writings of this remarkable man. I only wish the collection was longer or that some editor would ask me to do a preface for another book of this literary and spiritual quality.

Father Diele has picked the most poignant passages from the many writings of this profound Christian. He has arranged them according to the issues closest to Carlo Carretto's heart. These themes occur again and again in Carretto's books. They cover the most important ideas of the Christian faith inspired by Little Brother Carlo's unquenchable love. His life and writings breathe the fire of God's love — described by St. Paul in the thirteenth chapter of I Corinthians and in Jesus' description of God's love in the story of the prodigal father and his compassion to both younger brothers and elder brothers.

In his preface Father Diele sketches the life of Carretto. His life and his words are one. He knew the world. He was a professor, a leader in the Italian Catholic Youth Action movement and then a contemplative in the Sahara Desert joining the order founded by Charles de Foucauld. His passionate writing gradually drew attention to him, and he was invited to lecture in many cities as he traveled to visit the many fraternities of Little Brothers of Jesus. In his book *The Desert in the City*, he writes about how to live the contemplative life in the city. Toward the end of his life (he lived and wrote until his death in 1988), he and other Little Brothers set up a place of retreat where anyone could come to reflect, Christian or atheist, Moslem or Buddhist.

It is difficult not to be extravagant in one's praise of this collection of Carretto's reflections and meditations. Each page is a jewel. Together they contain the full gospel message — written as I have pointed out before — with literary genius and the fire of love.

Carretto sees the love of God everywhere in creation, in the rainbow and in the stones at his feet. He says poetically what John Polkinghorne, physicist-theologian, says in his recent Gifford Lectures, *Science and Christian Faith*. This universe was made so that human beings could emerge and know and experience the love of God and then share that love with God and all other human beings.

Creation was completed when the Holy One became a human being in the womb of Mary and was born as Jesus of Nazareth. One of Carlo's finest meditations reveals the courage and love of Mary who carried God into a hostile world and still stands with those who suffer tragedy of this fallen world.

Carretto speaks of prayer as a mutual interchange between the loving Creator and human beings who open themselves consciously to the Divine Lover. Here is authentic prayer at its best. Underlying his prayer is the knowledge that God is seeking us far more than we are seeking the Holy One. We can *know* the Divine as well as theologize about it. Indeed, theology that is not based on this experience is theology that has missed the mark. The third book of à Kempis' *Imitation of Christ* gives the same feeling of one who has lived in the presence of God and has dialogued with the risen and ascended Jesus. Carlo Carretto, however, has lived in our own era and struggled with our own global problems. He brings à Kempis into the twentieth century.

He knows the plight of women in most patriarchal societies. He has known the poor and suffering found all over our world. One of his most touching statements is that the crucified and risen Christ will be present as long as among us one suffering human being is left on our planet. The suffering Christ is particularly available to us in our human agony and pain.

Eucharist was for Carretto the place where we can most often and most fully touch the Kingdom of God. Jesus' first proclamation was "the reign of God is at hand and with us and available to us, the Divine fellowship and the company of heaven is around us and within us." In celebrating Eucharist we pause and take into us Christ's very life and being in the company of the host of heaven and our human neighbors. Once again Little Brother Carlo expresses for our age what à Kempis wrote for the fourteenth century in the fourth book of his classic; his reflections have been second only to the Bible in the number of copies printed. Carretto knew equally well the physical secular of poverty and glory and the spiritual world of bliss. At Eucharist these two worlds meet and we can see which one has eternal value.

The final words of this foreword need to be those of Carlo Carretto himself. They sum up his life and writing. In his book *In Search of the Beyond* (p. 133), he writes: "We evangelize with our lives before we do with our words ... Jesus came to bring fire not the catechism to the earth."

We can feel the fire of Carlo Carretto's love and of God's love as it burns through his life and words.

Morton Kelsey

Introduction

In this book of reflections I have attempted to present a sampling of the writings of one of the greatest contemporary spiritual thinkers, Carlo Carretto, Little Brother of the gospel. On my own spiritual pilgrimage I met the writings of Carlo Carretto back when I was in high school. I first read the book, *The God Who Comes*. Over the past twenty years Carretto has been for me a constant guide and companion. It was because of Carretto that I have discovered Charles de Foucauld and the spirituality that has most shaped my life, that is the spirituality of Jesus Caritas.

I remember the day I learned that Carlo Carretto died. I was very sad because I felt like I knew him and now was to live without this spiritual mentor.

For some of you this may be your first encounter with Carlo Carretto. Carlo was born on 2 April 1910 and was the third of six children. Four of the children of the Carretto family entered religious life. Growing up Carlo was most influenced by a Salesian Oratory located near the family home in a suburb of Turin. Carlo received degrees in history and philosophy. He taught and was very involved in the Catholic Action for Youth Movement, and in 1946 was elected its president. By the early fifties Carlo had gotten involved in many conflicts and had become disillusioned. He realized that he needed to resign from his post. He then began a spiritual search that by December 8, 1954 led him to enter the novitiate of the Little Brothers of Jesus, inspired by Charles de Foucauld. Carlo proceeded to live the life of a contemplative in the Sahara for ten years. He then spent time traveling to fraternities of Little Brothers in Turkey, France and Italy. In 1965 he went to Spello in Italy and eventually with his brothers created a place of welcome offering times of rest, prayer and solitude to both the believer and unbeliever. Over the years many would travel to spend time in the hermitages set up in Spello. Carlos' earthly journey came to an end on 4 October 1988 in his little cell at Spello.

We see in Brother Carlo a man who was a contemplative in the world living a life of action and contemplation and recognizing that in all things, at all times and in all persons the Divine Spirit was present.

In this collection I have chosen brief passages from the writings of Carlo Carretto for reflection. A good number of these pieces appear here in English for the first time. I have organized this book into seven chapters offering a means for one to use as a daily meditation through some of Carlo Carretto's writings. The struggle with us today is that life seems to be moving too fast and we don't find time for one another nor for God. Yet we are all called to be contemplative recognizing God in all persons, places and events of daily living.

In chapter 1, "And God Was Pleased," we are to meet the God who has created all. It is this creator God who is manifested in all of creation. We can say that creation is the first revelation of God. It is with the awareness that God creates and sustains the world that all people must do their part to tend the garden of God's creation.

In chapter 2, "And the Word Was Made Flesh," we are reminded that we, human creation, are the earth walking around with a conscience. What more can we do but praise God for the gift of our bodiliness and celebrate the fact that God is incarnate in the person of Jesus. God is among us in flesh and blood and so our flesh and the flesh of all persons is sacred.

When we have good news we want to tell others about it. It is because we have been so loved into creation that we must announce the gospel from the roof tops, with our very lives. In chapter 3, "Spread the Good News," the reflection turns toward sharing the Good News with the world. There is an excitement in sharing the Good News but also a challenge to act honestly.

We know that words by themselves do not convince a world that has too many words, that God is a reality. No, words by themselves in our society are too cheap. Actions are a sign and a witness to the world that we are true or false in what we profess with our lips. In chapter 4, "Hunger and Thirst for Justice," we are reminded that we must love with justice. We cannot stand back silently, or worse yet saying our prayers, and believe that the world would even consider the message we speak as true. We are thus called by the gospel we preach to respect the earth and to work for justice and peace.

In chapter 5, "This Is My Body, This Is My Blood," we are reminded that for the Christian the eucharist is the summit of who we say we are as believers. We are to be the Body of Christ in and for our world. If we are serious about our call then we know that we are to be contemplative in the world. The eucharist makes us one healed of all division. The very silence of the eucharist brings us into the silence of God. What more can we do but learn how to be still and sit at the master's feet and listen attentively. We are reminded by the eucharist that God alone is to be worshiped and adored. When we do this kind of adoration we live right and it becomes real to us that God is truly everywhere and in all persons.

To be contemplative is what we were made for and in the same breath we can say our one reason for living is to love. Love and contemplation are one and we are made to adore God through our thoughts, words and actions. Our very beings are to manifest the presence of God, discovering that God is everywhere at all times. The challenge of the contemplative life is taken up in chapter 6, "I Am with You Always."

In chapter 7, "I Am the Resurrection," we are reminded that we are not only made for contemplation and love but we were made to live forever. This chapter ends with a reflection in the form of a letter to us from Mary the mother of Jesus. She challenges us to believe in the resurrection and shows us how we can see even now in our lives the revelations of the resurrection. Mary is the first of the disciples who knows that God is the God of the impossible and that selfless love is our destiny. In Mary we see faith made real as she embraced the call of the angel. It is revealed to us that God is transforming the earth and each person willing to be changed from pain to healing, from sin to mercy, from fear to security, from weakness to strength and from death into life.

My hope is that in this collection of meditations you will meet Carlo Carretto and as he has done for so many others, he will point you in the direction of Jesus.

And God Was Pleased

We live in a time when people are again realizing that God has offered us the earth as a garden for us to tend. The earth belongs to God and everything on it is God's. We can look at our earth and recall that the earth is God's first revelation to us. Brother Carlo reminds us that the earth is God's gift to us. We praise God for the earth and we praise God through all of creation.

God Can Do Everything

One of the most profound concepts that constantly surfaces from this letter called Bible, which God wrote throughout the centuries to humankind, is the following: "I, the living God, the Almighty, am the only thing you need, my child. Why are you searching for idols that do not see and do not or cannot feel? Why do you set your hopes on those who cannot help you? Trust me alone . . . and you will see!" And God calls us and establishes with us the most intimate relationship of confidence and trust. We could reduce our entire life to a single act of faith. Jesus himself demanded this act of faith whenever he performed miracles. Can you believe? All right: "Your faith has saved you" (Mk 10:52).

The more we get used to thinking that God can do everything, the more we approach the truth and partake in the extraordinary and sweetest alliance with God. And as the Saints proclaimed, with such an ally . . . none of our enemies will be able to resist.

(*Ogni Giorno un Pensiero*, p. 242)

Called To Be
Co-Creators With God

Here is the miracle of love: to discover that all creation is one, flung out into space by a God who is a Father, and that if you present yourself to it as he does — unarmed, and full of peace — creation will recognize you and meet you with a smile.

(*I, Francis*, p. 75)

Non-violence regards first of all nature, the skies, the seas, the mines, the forests, the air, water, the home.

These are the first objects of non-violence. It is a terrible sin you have committed all around you, and I do not know whether or not you can still be saved.

You have violated the forests, defiled the seas, plundered everything like a bunch of bandits. Your contempt for nature knows no bounds.

If there were a court of the skies, or for the seas, or of mines, you would all of you (or almost all) be under sentence of death.

And perhaps there is such a court. An invisible one. For your punishment has certainly begun.

You can scarcely breathe your air. Your food has become unhealthy. Cancer assaults you with more and more regularity.

(*I, Francis*, p. 76)

God is in nature, God is in matter: matter is divinized, vivified, by God's presence. Now that I know these things I no longer kick stones about as I used to as a child; I have a greater understanding of the Orientals who wish never to do violence to nature because they respect it too much as mediating God's presence.

Perhaps the medievals' love of and attachment to the divine transcendence has helped us forget that God is also immanent, that he is everywhere. It has created in the past a western religious concept which takes little or no account of natural realities, sees no connection between God and plants, between God and animals around us.

I shall never forget a group of schoolboys waiting at a station in the May sunshine throwing stones at the lizards and throwing the lizards with a laugh on the fire. Such things are relics of a time when a supposed love of God saw no connection with a love of nature and created people, even religious, who saw nothing wrong with hunting, and by that I mean not catching a hare or a pheasant for the family to eat, but the brutal joy of seeing game twitch under the shower of lead.

(*Love is for Living*, p. 85)

All Creation Is Charged with the Grandeur of God

There is no creature, thing, thought or idea which does not speak to me of him and which is not a message from him. "Up, up to the outermost point of the universe and down, down to the utter limits of my own nothingness, I see him."

The entire universe is a Sacred Host which contains him, speaks to me of him and in which I adore him as both immanent and transcendent, the root of my being, my beginning, support and final end: as *he who is*.

God is the sea in which I swim, the atmosphere in which I breathe, the reality in which I move.

I cannot find the tiniest thing which does not speak to me of him, which is not somehow his image, his message, his call, his smile, his reproach, his word.

(*Love is for Living*, p. 19)

The Hand of the Artist
Is in All That Has Been Made

So much light!

And how easy it is to witness to the light! It is the priestly function of us as humans. Upright on earth, I feel that the creatures turn to me so that I can voice their silent adoration of God.

The wind, the fire, the dew and the forest, the ice and the snow, the mountains and the hills, the springs and the seas press on me from all sides. They seem to say: You must not fail your vocation to speak for us all in the sight of God.

(Love is for Living, p. 23)

Is there any creature which does not speak to us of him? Which is not his photograph and symbol? Which is not an invitation from him?

Are we not immersed in the sublime, in the immense, in the beautiful, in the perfect, dreaming the most extraordinary dream? Are we not part of an infinite multiplicity continually being reduced to the most fantastic unity? If we look through creation, do we not see God?

Is not the immensity of the universe an image of his immensity?

Is not he, and only he, the reply to all our questions?

Yes, he is, most definitely!

(Love is for Living, p. 28)

The Road to God Is
the Road on Which We Walk Now

You should feel and see the creatures, every creature.

Why take such an interest in a dewdrop appearing on the Virgin's eyelash in a painting, yet not see all the dewdrops of a morning in spring?

Why go miles and miles to see the dubious stigmata on someone or other's hands, yet not move a step to contemplate the sore-covered hands of the poor?

Begin feeling God in creatures. See his beauty in the beauty of the sun as it rises on your human day. Hear his voice in the voice of the brother beside you, trying to communicate with you.

Waste no more time, seeking God in your own fantasies.

Once you realize how miraculous it is that a bee can find the door of its hive, you will feel that God is near you and near your silence.

Try and sing.

For the sky that you have given us, alleluia!

For the sun that you have given us, alleluia!

For the sea that you have given us, alleluia!

For the friends that you have given us, alleluia!

Yes, alleluia, even if the sky is sometimes stormy.

Alleluia, even if the sun is sometimes scorching.

Alleluia, even if your friends do not always see eye to eye with you.

All is grace.

All is God, loving me.

God is in all, molding me.

God is in all, making me his son.

(*Summoned by Love*, p. 60)

Yes, today this is no longer a secret for me: human experience is already experience of God.

Our journey on earth is already a journey to heaven. Seeing a sunrise or a flower is already seeing God.

Discovering a galaxy with a telescope is a way of approaching your littleness to his greatness; basking in a sunny flowering meadow is to glimpse the garment of the eternal.

When I fall in love with something or someone, I feel God's call, and when I am eaten up with insatiability inspired in me by some creature, I realize that God alone is the Absolute.

Know, that it is no longer secret, to seek to know God by experience, since all knowledge is experience of him.

(*I Sought and Found God*, p. 60)

Going Beyond

God molds and touches me through created things and little by little makes me aware by the gentleness of his grace and the strength of his Spirit.

I am inside things, am made of things, but aspire to a life transcending things.

Born into things as son of man, I am becoming son of God.

Born the first time of my father and mother who gave me the earthly realities, I shall be born a second time as a son of the heavenly realities.

Now I am like an immature fetus, midway between my past and future, between the things I know and those I do not know.

It isn't a comfortable situation.

In fact it hurts.

I suffer from incompleteness, from blindness, from yearning.

From incompleteness, because I have not yet been made and I sin by reason of my immaturity; from blindness, because I cannot see clearly since thus enclosed in things; from yearning, because I already have the blood of God in my veins and have patiently to put up with my own sick, turbulent, human blood.

Were I to be told that I had to stay in this situation forever, I should think it very bad news.

That would be like being told, "You must stay in your mother's womb forever."

I love my mother's womb, where I was generated, but I emerged from it as soon as I could; I would rather look at my mother from outside, not from inside.

(*Summoned by Love*, p. 24)

And the Word Is Made Flesh

Somewhere in the beginning of time as we know it, God made us, male and female we were made. We are made in God's image and we are endowed with God's Spirit.

We are embodied spirits, enfleshed in time and destined for eternity. Over and again we are reminded that we are flesh and blood. As babies we cry for food and drink; we are ever seeking the gentle embrace of a mother. As we grow, we discover what the word hot means and we even learn that when we are cut we bleed. What we discover is that we are flesh that has been God touched.

"And the word became flesh and lives among us." God is in our midst in the flesh, making all flesh sacred. Our sexuality, our very maleness and femaleness remind us that we are humans who have the divine within us. All that is sexual, all that is flesh is sacred because God is among us in the here and now in our flesh.

31

We Are Completely Incomplete

As always in the Bible, the truth is concealed beneath symbols and signs of words. Adam's sleep is like an ecstasy in which the man sees and loves and desires the creature for whom he searches and whom God himself offers, the creature who suits him, who will complete him, who will gladden him, who will help him to make the most of himself.

And waking up he sees this creature and exclaims: "This at last is bone from my bones, and flesh from my flesh" (Gn 2:23). The biblical account of the creation of woman reads almost like a children's story. It is one, in fact, because basically the human will always be "God's child," and here it is God talking. But it has such a ring of truth about it that beyond the signs of the words there lies the mystery of the deep, unbreakable union of man and woman.

It is God's intention that they should be "chips off the same block," so that metaphysically man will not be able to say to a woman: "Go away, I don't know you, you and I don't belong together."

No, he will always have to say: "Bone from my bones, flesh from my flesh" and remain with her; so long as life lasts, he cannot separate himself from his own flesh. Man therefore must be united with his wife: God wanted it to be like this, and so should we.

(*Love is for Living*, p. 60)

Woman completes man, and man woman. Love fulfills them, makes them better, introduces them more easily into the divine stream of charity, forces them to become open, transforms them.

And it also makes them fruitful. We have said that fecundity is stamped into the nature of things as a sign of God's creativeness, and human beings are no exception.

(Love is for Living, p. 62)

The purpose of marriage, however, is not only to give birth to children — although that on its own is a thing of divine beauty. It is also designed to fulfill the marriage partners. The matrimonial union does not concern only the generation to come; it should also be seen as a divinely willed means to fulfil, reconcile, cheer, sustain, improve the man and the woman. This fulfillment is brought by love, it is realized in love.

Here we could apply Augustine's famous "love and do what you like," in the certainty that if the partners really love each other they will find in their mutual relationship the path, the pointer, the ladder to another love which should develop in every creature on earth and take it later to perfect union with God. I should say that matrimonial love — for those whose vocation is marriage, that is for most of mankind — is the beginning, the pattern, the blueprint, of love for the absolute in which, beyond time, we shall all be absorbed.

Marriage partners who love each other find that love synthesizes their relationship. Life together becomes easy in love; it becomes easy to understand, bear with and excuse each other. It even becomes easy to sacrifice oneself for the other.

Love in marriage ultimately helps men and women to leave the dark cave of their egoism and the constant danger of returning to themselves and to become open to creation and so to God. I have seen impossible young men — timid, introvert, unmanageable — suddenly become gentle, open altruists in the warmth of a girlfriend's love. It is like seeing a dead branch fill with sap and bud at the approach of spring. Love is an all-the-year-round spring!

We can never sufficiently express the benefits of love, especially on the sick, the timid, pessimists, egoists, difficult cases.

No medicine is so powerful as genuine love.

Everything mends and comes to life; and instead of lapsing into an empty, sterile melancholy, we set off with enthusiasm as if life had started to flow through our veins again.

Saved by love, we find in it the joy of life, application to our work, dedication to an ideal, and under its inspiration we can at last devote our lives to something worthwhile!

Love, truth, is God's finger laid on a person's heart.

(Love is for Living, p. 64)

The Divine Feminine

Strange. I have asked myself many times how it is possible that, in spite of personages as remarkable as Clare, as Catherine, as Teresa, you in the Church are still so anti-feminist?

Yes, I have to say it, I, Francis, You are still so anti-feminist.

I cannot understand!

Have you fear of a woman because a woman endangers your virtue? Or do you consider her, without openly saying so, as belonging to an inferior race, unworthy to touch the holy things?

Are you still the slaves of ancient cultures, in which a woman was of no account, in which she was subjugated by male arrogance and destined only to live behind a curtain like the women of the Muslims?

One would say that you have no prophecy, that you have no truth to proclaim. Above all one would say that you are still living in the past.

(*I, Francis*, p. 39)

I should like to keep quite still, so as not to lose the changing impact of this thought. Woman completes man, man completes woman: woman is complementary to man's personality, man is complementary to hers. Unity is achieved in this mysterious "work" of God's, when man seeks woman as part of himself and in the ecstasy of love says, "You are bone of my bones and flesh of my flesh." Then that unity will be complete, and beautiful and fruitful and delightful and soothing, since willed by God.

(*Made in Heaven*, p. 20)

Love Without Grasping, Needing, Holding On

Today I would translate Jesus' words, "Blessed are the pure in heart" as, "Blessed is the one who knows how to embrace chastely the entire universe."

Jesus did not come in order to add to our burdens, he came to set us free; he did not come to deprive us of that embrace, but to make it chaste.

To be pure is to embrace things chastely; to be impure is to embrace them in a lustful way, defiling them, violating them and prostituting them in the process. Is that not true?

A man embraces his own wife chastely, but not the woman he buys by exerting his male superiority.

We embrace our work chastely, and our house acquired honestly, our toil and our friendships, but not our thefts, our arrogance, our blasphemies, our insincerity or our intolerance.

There is a vast difference between a husband's creative embrace, and the functional embrace of the soldier of fortune who breaks in the doors of the vanquished and rapes the first woman he meets.

As soon as we really understand that Jesus did not come to deny us love and union, but to raise them to a new level for us, making them even more beautiful, more human, more joyful, more authentic, we will have taken a great step forward in our understanding of the gospel. But often, only too often, we want to try things out in our own way, and nine times out of ten, our misfortunes stem from this desire of ours to "try" from this practical if not theoretical denial of the law which God gave us out of love.

(*In Search of the Beyond*, p. 178)

I can feel enthusiastic about a Church where every man has one wife and only one, where there is no divorce and everything happens in an orderly way. But as soon as I become aware that this is imposed by civil law then I rebel because I feel my freedom is destroyed.

Not even God has imposed celibacy on man and the chastity of having only one wife (his friend Abraham had two, and his forebear David had . . . eleven).

The absolute of chastity is something so lofty and so closely linked to love as to halt even God on the threshold of the human person's "yes."

How crude are certain discourses concerning the unity of marriage based on the law and delivered by Christians who remember all about Jesus apart from the Beatitudes.

And that's quite a lot!

Which doesn't mean that it is impossible to discourse on chastity and marital union and the respect for life.

Indeed I can do this and I must. But in a suitable setting.

And if I appeal to civil law I do so as a citizen who respects the multiplicity of cultures and the authentic difficulties of humanity's story as living a life not yet permeated by the gospel.

And above all, in order to leave everyone free, I vote for minorities and try not to impose my religious ideas through the strength of numbers.

But if I appeal to divine law, the law which Jesus has implanted in my heart and for loyalty to which I am prepared to die, then I change my tone and say:

Brothers and sisters!

God in his son Jesus has freed us from the dark powers of paganism, of permissiveness, of money of Eastern and Western materialism, and has arranged for us to live in his kingdom of light and love.

We are not like those who do not believe in Christ's resurrection and who live as if invisible things did not exist.

Through God's mercy we believe in Jesus risen from the dead, and from him we draw the strength to live on this earth as he has taught us in the gospel.

Others may divorce, but not us.

Other woman may have abortions through weakness or ignorance or power, but not our women because we believe in life.

For us love isn't the embrace of a body but a total gift of ourselves to a creature whom we love as God loves us and whom we cannot deceive at any moment.

This way of loving binds us to chaste living which is not easy, indeed it would be impossible if we were not already "risen in Christ" and if we did not obtain help through our prayer.

We do not impose chastity on others but we want to live it ourselves as testimony that we believe in the invisible God who lives in each one of us and who calls us to freedom and salvation.

To be chaste means to respect our own body and the body of others.

To be chaste means to look on others with the eyes of a child, believing that true love is possible, that on this earth the marvel will never vanish of a boy and girl capable of giving themselves totally, radically, for ever, as if their love were already a piece of heaven.

To be chaste means to have control over oneself for it cannot happen that our child is the fruit of casual fornication but of loving and conscientious fatherhood and motherhood, accepted as a free choice and with a joy embedded in the very mystery of God.

To be chaste means to see things with the pure eyes of Jesus who, in his messianic vision, wanted the whole universe to be drawn into the dazzling potency of the resurrection in which our very sin would be conquered, destroyed and forgotten.

And, finally, to be chaste means to have in our hearts the dream of Mary, Mother of Christ and our mother, who in her infinite smallness and humility was able to live the requirements of virginity and motherhood at the same time and in the same body.

(*The Desert in the City*, p. 104)

Spread the Good News

In our day it seems so easy to tell of all the many tragedies that happen both near and far. It seems that pain and non-truth flows like a mighty rushing waterfall. Yet we have heard with our own ears and seen with our own eyes that God is in our land. God walks among us.

Time and again we are reminded of our fragile natures. We are reminded through our lived experience that we are small, a speck in the universe. We so often feel we are just dust amid the many galaxies. Yet God is with us. We do matter and we have not been forgotten, this is Good News.

What else can we do but shout about this Good News from the roof tops, God loves us. To the ends of the earth we must go telling everyone along the roads of life that we are loved. Here we stand a speck in the universe but a loved speck, not some hapless accident of time but rather loved into being. It is this Good News that we announce far and wide, day in and day out, God is with us.

Just Learn to Be Brother, to Be Sister, to the Human Family

You may pass on the fruits of your contemplation, not your wisdom, or worse still, your culture.

Only when we contemplate the face of God, and are carried beyond ourselves in so doing, can we effectively say to our neighbor: come and see, and understand for yourself how sublime God is!

To lead others to contemplation: that is the soul of every apostolate. Come and see, come and try for yourself, come and experience, come with me to the holy mountain.

What persuades your brother and sister to follow you is the grace of God, which is never lacking, and your own conviction, your experience, your example — of which there can never be too much.

(In Search of the Beyond, p. 134)

We evangelize with our lives before we do so with our words.

Anyone who reduces the gospel to a formula will be an efficient administrator, but a prophet, never.

Jesus came to bring fire not the catechism to the earth.

If we are content to catechize, without announcing the Good News in our own lives, we will find we are writing in the sand, which the wind of passion will carry away. The mounds upon mounds of catechisms that have been turned inside out in our parishes and chewed over in seminaries have helped to produce the present crisis in which everything is known about Christ and about the Church, but no one any longer believes either in the Church or in Christ. The catechism, without life and without witness, is like medicine given to a dead person.

(*In Search of the Beyond*, p. 133)

Here Is the One Whose Breath We Breathe

The experience of God's presence in nature and in history for me is fundamental.

It is the substance of faith.

Gradually I must arrive at living it, at feeling it by day and by night, being aware of it when I work and when I rest, enjoying it when I pray and when I love.

Always!

Twenty-four hours out of twenty-four!

It is the path that leads me to live in the kingdom of God which is the union between heaven and earth, between God and humanity.

But let us understand each other: it is not a matter of establishing the union with God on our side. Because the union exists; it already existed before I was aware of it.

That is an absolute because nothing exists outside of God.

In God we live and move and have our being (Acts 17:28); this is the basis of all reality, the explanation of being, the very significance of Life, the enduring root of Love.

What matters on our side is to become aware of this union, to be attentive to it in faith, to deepen it in hope, to live in charity.

It is the story of the baby who gradually discovers its mother and father, of the woman who finds her husband, of the man who finds a friend.

But the mother and father were there already, the husband was there already, the friend was there already.

And God was there already. It is for us to discover him within ourselves, not to create him.

God's presence in ourselves, in the cosmos in the invisible, in everything, is basic. You will never be in any place, in any situation, where he is not.

O Lord, thou has searched me and know me!

Thou knowest when I sit down and when I rise up;

Thou discoverest my thoughts from afar,

Thou searchest out my path and my lying down . . .

And it is silly to think that he is in church and not in the street, that he is in the Sacrament and not in the crowd, that he is in happiness and not in sorrow, in bright, kind things and not on storms and earthquakes.

(*The Desert in the City*, p. 27)

Who Can Know the Mind of God?

When I left for the desert I left everything behind me as Jesus had asked me to — I left family, house, money, situation. The only thing I didn't leave were my ideas about God which were all packed into a big book about theology, and this book I took with me.

And there on the sand I went on reading and re-reading this book as if God were contained in an idea and as if I could communicate with him because I had fine ideas about him.

My novice-master said to me, "Brother Carlo, leave those books alone. Put yourself stripped and humble in front of the eucharist. Empty yourself, de-intellectualize yourself, try to love, try to contemplate..."

But I didn't understand a word of what he was trying to say to me. I remained thoroughly anchored to my ideas.

So he thought it would help me to empty myself, and to understand, if he sent me to work.

My goodness!

It isn't easy to work in those oases in the heat of the day!

When I returned to the fraternity I felt absolutely whacked, all my strength drained out of me.

I collapsed onto the matting in front of the Sacrament in the chapel, my head aching, my back breaking. And all my ideas flew away like birds flying from an open cage.

I couldn't even start to pray. I was arid, empty, exhausted. The only thing that came from my mouth was a groan.

The only positive thing that I felt, and that I began to understand, was solidarity with the poor, the truly poor, with anyone crushed under the weight of the daily yoke, with anyone on the assembly line. And I thought of my mother praying with five children around her feet, and of the peasants who had to work a twelve-hour day in the summer.

If peace and quite were a prerequisite of prayer, then those poor people wouldn't have ever been able to pray. So evidently the prayer I had abundantly practiced up till then was the prayer of the rich, the prayer of comfortable well-fed people who were masters of their own timetable.

I no longer understood anything, or rather I was beginning to understand a great deal.

I wept!

My tears fell on the overall that was the mark of my poor person's toil.

And it was in that state of authentic poverty that I made the most important discovery of my life of prayer.

Do you want to know what it was?

That prayer takes place in the heart, not in the head.

(*The Desert in the City*, p. 22)

I shall tell you something else which is very important for busy people like you who say they have no time to pray.

Try to look at the reality in which you live — your work, your commitments, your relationships, your meetings, your walks, the shopping, the newspapers, the children — as a single whole from which you cannot disengage yourself, a whole which you have to think about.

I shall say more: a whole by means of which God speaks to you and through which he guides you.

So it is not by fleeing that you will find God more easily, but it is by changing your heart that you see things differently.

The desert in the city is only possible on these terms: that you see things with a new eye, touch them with a new spirit, love them with a new heart.

(*The Desert in the City*, p. 21)

Live the Gospel Everywhere

It was on the seventeenth floor of a huge block of workers' apartments that I had arranged to meet some of my young Chinese friends.

We had been talking for hours — about the gospel, about commitment, about prayer.

Then a student of architecture who lived in Hong Kong (though his parents lived in the People's Republic near Shanghai) suddenly said: "Brother Carlo, I have been wanting to meet you ever since I read your *Letters from the Desert*. You write so enthusiastically about the time you spent in the Sahara that one gets the impression that there's no substitute for that kind of solitude. But I can't go there. I must find my God here in the Babel of my city. So what do you advise me to do? How should I set about it? Is it possible? And if it is possible, why don't you write a book for us to help us find our desert here in the city?

"And don't forget China."

I felt deeply moved and at the same time deeply understood.

The young student looked at me with sympathy.

And that was the moment when *The Desert in the City* was born in my heart.

Outside the window it was evening and I saw the great mass of Hong Kong's skyscrapers switching on their lights.

I remembered that I had seen this sight for the first time in New York — skyscrapers with all their lights on. Illuminated skyscrapers look like diamonds.

It seems impossible that such ugly objects should become alive and beautiful when clothed with light.

So there's nothing that is altogether negative. Even the city, sink of iniquity and asphalt jungle, can have its light and its "transparency."

"The desert in the city," I repeated over and over to myself, looking out of the window, my thoughts reaching to the distant origin of this word "desert" which had been laid on my heart at the best moment of my life. I thought back to nights in the Sahara, to the sand dunes, to all the paths I had trodden to the search for intimacy with God, to the memorable stars which decorated so discreetly the sweetness of the African nights, deep symbol as they were of the nights in which my faith was immersed and in which I felt so well and so safe.

The real desert, the desert of sand and stars, had been my first love, and I would never have left it had not obedience claimed me from afar.

"Brother Carlo, you have discovered the absolute of God, now you must discover the absolute of man."

So off I had gone in search of people.

I was thoroughly disoriented and it took me

some time to recover my equilibrium and deep joy.

But then God caused me to realize that there was no privileged "place" where he lived but that everywhere was the "place" where he lived and that you could find him anywhere.

(*The Desert in the City*, p. 14)

And in just such a way God, who is "surprise," has now brought me to China. The surprise did not lie in my having to make another journey; no, I have made plenty of journeys. The novelty lay in the fact that I did not expect it, and least of all did I expect what he wanted to tell me here in Hong Kong, in this city so like and yet so unlike other cities, and at that vast airport. For at that vast airport people arrive from all the continents of the world, and trade on a world scale is able to make the Chinese from the People's Republic exchange smiles with the Chinese from Formosa; while Japanese, Koreans, Americans, Europeans, Arabs and Indians assemble in the same skyscraper and are all ready to smile if only they can do good business.

Mao Tse-tung said: "In Hong Kong hens lay golden eggs," and this is why he maintained it as it was with a special statute even though — had he so wished — he would have occupied it in a few hours.

Hong Kong struck me as being a true city of the future, riding at anchor on limitless waters and with streets improbably scattered with temples dedicated to idols, as were the streets of Corinth and Athens at the time of St. Paul. The names of the temples are as follows: The Bank of America, The Hong Kong-Shanghai Banking Corporation, The Bank of China, The Chartered Bank, The Bank of Tokyo, La Banque Nationale de Paris, The Dresner Bank, The Chase Manhattan Bank, The Hang Seng Bank, the Bank of Bangkok, The Amsterdam Bank, and so on.

It is a pity that these temples all have the same kind of facade and there is no scope of the imagination in the modern idolatry.

But perhaps it is precisely because these temples lack imagination and fantasy that I have been able to find my greatest surprise among the young people of China.

Let me explain.

Knowing about my arrival in Hong Kong, a group of friends had been kind enough to translate my *Letters from the Desert* into Chinese-Cantonese and to get them serialized in the local papers. I don't know how they managed it. All I know is that on my arrival I was besieged by my readers. Nothing of the kind had ever happened to me before. Night and day I was inundated by telephone calls, invitations, requests to address meetings, and so on.

And the theme was always the same: the gospel of Jesus.

I still see before me the bright eyes of the young Chinese who questioned me passionately on the subject of Christ.

So obviously the temples with their pagan idols had not won over everyone. The spirit of the Lord had breathed on the young workers and intellectuals and students with whom I came into contact and had raised questions in their minds, questions about invisible realities, about the meaning of existence and the purpose of life.

Brother Carlo, tell me how to pray.

Tell me how to think about God's presence in the world. What does God's "kingdom" mean? How can I live the Beatitudes?

More than anything it was the gospel that stirred them. These young people, educated in one or other of the various religions of Hong Kong, sensed the oldness of their catechisms, the static quality of their practices, the immobility of their institutions.

It was obvious that they were dissatisfied.

They wanted to hear a new message, and this was to be found in the gospel of Jesus.

(*The Desert in the City*, p. 10)

As I prepare to speak about community, about our task in the contemporary world and our apostolate to our fellow persons, I would like to sum it all up in a famous phrase of Raissa Maritain: "contemplation in the market place."

And I also want to emphasize that there exists no human preparation for the task of evangelization, or if there does, it is within the framework of God's plan, which nearly always eludes us.

But what does exist, as something we are all capable of grasping, is the fact that for each one of us evangelization is but the reflection of the light of the Beatitudes, which shines in our faces with increasing intensity as we draw near to Jesus, the divine model. To everyone who is living in darkness, evangelization comes like the moon, rising above the darkness of his or her way. But moonlight is always the reflection of the original source of light — the sun.

Christ is the sun of the earth, and in everyone's night someone or something is needed to reflect his light, someone who has already absorbed it. Ensuring that the light of Jesus is a living reality within you is the one indispensable condition on which your ability to shed light on someone else who is close to you depends.

If you want to be an apostle, do not look around for something else. Your wisdom does not matter; only your capacity to absorb the light of God that comes to you in Christ matters.

(*In Search of the Beyond*, p. 134)

Cry the Gospel with Your Life

To take to one's prayers when the village is burning and the inhabitants crying for help is to create an untenable excuse for one's own laziness and one's own fear.

That is why a Church that concentrates on its own ritual and is not aware of the sufferings and anxieties of people, of the chains that bind them, is a dead Church, with nothing more to say about the heart and mind of its founder.

That is why the scandal of piety based on processions, masses for the dead, and private devotional practices unrelated to the evangelization of the poor, gets swept to one side by the protest of those who still believe in the inexorable power of the word of God.

(*In Search of the Beyond*, p. 131)

Hunger and Thirst for Justice

Justice is seeing as God sees. There is much suffering, pain and misery in our world, yet we are the people of God, a people of hope. We dream the dream of God who is the master of all that is impossible. We therefore dream the impossible dream of God; a world where justice is a reality. The scriptures tell us that God dreams of a new heaven and a new earth and so do we.

As people of the kingdom we seek justice in a world that does not always seem open to God or God's just ways.

There is a story told of the people of a village who notice day after day dead bodies floating past their village on the river. Day after day these good and faithful people bring in the bodies and bury them. Charity surely abounds in this village where the dead are buried as an act of mercy. One day someone comes along and says, "and where are these bodies coming from and what has happened to these people?" On that day the village has begun to do the work of justice. If we do the work of God's kingdom then we are involved in not only the works of charity, but also the works of justice. In short it means we have begun to dream the dream of God.

Walk with the Poor

Today the poor are a real cause for scandal; to be rid of this scandal it would be better to spend less time arguing about the nature of chastity and put more emphasis on this beatitude which is in danger of being forgotten by those who are trying to "live as Christians." If it is true, as it is, that the perfection of the law is love, then it must fully control my desire for possessions and riches. Otherwise I shall not know what the beatitude really means.

If I love, if I really love, how can I tolerate the fact that a third of humanity is menaced with starvation while I enjoy the security of economic stability? If I act in that way I shall perhaps be a good Christian, but I shall certainly not be a saint; and today there are far too many good Christians, when the world need saints. We must learn to accept instability, put ourselves every now and then in the condition of having to say, "Give us this day our daily bread," with real anxiety because the larder is empty; have the courage, for love of God and one's neighbor, to give until it hurts and, above all, keep open in the wall of the soul the great window of living faith in the providence of an all-powerful God.

I know that what I have said about poverty is challenging, and I also know that when I was in the world I did not really put it into practice. It is I who have lived for years behind the mask of "pleasing others"; it is I who have spent money, and not only my own, on things which are "not real."

And yet, in spite of this, I cannot remain silent; and to my friends I must say: beware of the temptation of riches. It is much more serious than it may appear today to well-intentioned Christians, and it sows destruction primarily because we underestimate its danger.

Riches are a slow poison, which strikes almost imperceptibly, paralyzing the soul at the moment when it seems healthiest. They are thorns which grow with the grain and suffocate it right at the moment when the corn is beginning to shoot up. What a number of men and women, religious people, let themselves get caught up in their later lives by the spirit of middle-class tastes.

(*Letters from the Desert*, p. 80)

Poverty means love for Jesus, the poor par excellence. It involves the voluntary acceptance of a limitation. Jesus wished to be poor in order to share the limitations of the poor, to experience in himself the crude reality weighing upon those who toil for their daily bread, to experience in his spirit the anguishing uncertainty of those who own nothing. The gospel praises such poverty practiced for love.

(*Ogni Giorno un Pensiero*, p. 50)

The struggle against injustice and outrages, especially those committed against the poor and defenseless, is basic Christianity, and Christians are not permitted to be silent, to withdraw, to refuse to get involved.

If they understood, really understood, they would volunteer to die for justice.

That is what Jesus did.

But nowhere is it written that to make your adversary yield it is necessary or indispensable to employ the sword, the machine gun, or the tank.

The highest claim of the gospel is that I can cause my enemy to yield with my unarmed love, with my bare hand, as Gandhi did, as Martin Luther King did, as all who believe in non-violence do, as Bishop Romero did in your times.

What a sublime example this unarmed person gave! What wonderful words he spoke against the arrogant, who massacred his people!

Give a nation a handful of men and women like that — give the Church a band of heroes of strength like that — and then you will realize that when Jesus proposed non-violence he was not doing so in order to lose battles. He was doing so in order to win them, and win them in the only way worthy of a human being: without shedding the blood of others, but by shedding one's own.

This is the principle of martyrdom, which has never been lacking in the Church and which is the highest witness a human being can bear upon earth.

Further than that one cannot go.

(I, Francis, p. 25)

Take Nothing for the Journey

Here is the miracle of love: to discover that all creation is one, flung out into space by a God who is a Father, and that if you present yourself to it as he does — unarmed, and full of peace — creation will recognize you and meet you with a smile.

This is the principle of non-violence, and I should like to recommend it to you with all the enthusiasm of which I am capable.

I have asked you not to speak over much of poverty today. Your environment is too ambiguous in its regard, and it is too difficult to explain your position in your bourgeois and socialist milieu. Instead, I tell you this, and I tell you most emphatically: Speak of non-violence, be apostles of non-violence, become non-violent.

Now is the hour to do so, in fact it may be the last hour, inasmuch as you are all sitting on top of a stockpile of bombs, and you can blow up at any moment now.

(*I, Francis*, p. 75)

Because it could be — and it happens — that while I am in the drawing room after a sumptuous dinner discussing the burning problems of Portuguese colonialism, I forget my wife or my mother all alone in the kitchen, washing the dishes from the feast with my sophisticated friends. Is the spirit of colonialism not at the bottom of our hearts?

Because maybe — and it happens — that at the same moment I am hurling myself furiously against the sins committed by the racist pride of whites against blacks, I find I am the kind of person who is always right, who tells his father he understands nothing because he is a poor peasant, who burns a little incense daily before the idol who has had the good fortune to be a "manager," a "boss," "clerk," a "teacher," or if I am a woman, a "beautiful body."

Then I remember the words of Jesus: "If you want to avoid judgment, stop passing judgment. Your verdict on others will be the verdict passed on you. The measure with which you measure will be used to measure you" (Mt 7:1-2).

(*The God Who Comes*, p. 188)

The tree of love is not the tree of social justice (often it is that as well, but not always), or the tree of philanthropy; even less is it the tree of the arrogant display of one who wants to prove to me that he is better or more generous than others.

The tree of love is the tree of love, and only someone who loves can appreciate that and live the life of evangelical poverty. Poverty without love is a form of mutilation, not a blessing.

Which explains why I must begin to love before I set out to solve the problem of poverty.

Yes, that is where I must start. I must love my fellow men and women, love them until I really grasp that they are my fellow men and women, my equals. Once I have learned to love them with a love that is true, authentic and uncalculating, such love will lead me on to ever greater heights. But first it will lead me downwards. Step by step it will force me to come down from the heights of my presumption until I reach the humble level of equality. Slowly but surely it will rid me of the arrogant conviction that I am better, more intelligent, more gifted than my neighbor. It will strip the mast of social conviction from my face, destroy my false family or racial values — my belief that my skin is fairer, my blood more distinguished, my culture older, my religion better founded.

That is how I will become poor, poor in spirit first of all, poor in heart.

(In Search of the Beyond, p. 144)

This first Beatitude of Jesus preached in his sermon on the mount is so all-embracing and the heedless Christians of our age have reduced it to such mean, unattractive "charity."

The poor are not simply those who are aware of limits to their own material wealth; over and above this, they are the ones who set bounds to their own spiritual pride and surround their hearts with barbed wire, as it were, to safeguard it from the vanity of useless and dangerous affections.

Because — and let us be quite clear about this — if the possession of capital riches is ugly in people who exclude their brothers and sisters from the feast, much more ugly is that spiritual wealth which encourages the idea that whites are superior to blacks and keeps them away from the table of the God-given equality of humanity. Those who are proud and spiritually rich cause more hurt than those who are rich in money and material goods. There is no limit to the presumption, to the complacency and sense of superiority that exudes from the expression of someone who is convinced that all truth and culture belong to him or her. The gospel is less sympathetically disposed to these riches of mind and heart, and Jesus' words "Woe to you who are rich" sound a far more serious and warning note for the "wise" of this world than for the man who, by defrauding his brothers, buys a larger vineyard than he actually needs.

Go to the universities, go to the centers of culture, to the clubs where men and women assume the title of "master." Go into the political circles, move among those who feel they are invested with the divine mission to command, to promulgate laws, to interpret the truth.

Go with your New Testament in your pocket. You will be sickened by all this spiritual and intellectual pride, this struggle to get ahead regardless of anyone else, this lust for possessions.

There is one category of people whose arrogance exceeds that of all others: self-confident religious people who act as proprietors of religion; who, instead of serving, make use of divine things for their own ends, and instead of taking the last places, force their way up to the first, raining down the deadly blows of their abused power as they go (cf. Mt 23).

It is not insignificant that Jesus was killed by a clique of this kind; that he felt, almost to the point of despair, that as far as the Pharisees of the Temple were concerned his message was a dead letter from the moment he uttered it.

And let us bear in mind that each one of us has it in us to become a Pharisee, capable of crucifying Jesus anew in our own hearts, as long as we forget to be poor, poor, poor.

(*In Search of the Beyond*, p. 142)

Your Kingdom Come

Where there is hate, let there be your love
Where there is war, let there be peace
Where there is uncleanness, let there be purity
Where there is lust, let there be chastity
Where there is violence, let there be meekness
Where there is vengeance, let there be forgiveness
Where there is wealth, let there be charity
Where there is poverty, let there be
    joyful acceptance
Where there is terror, let there be tranquility
Where there is fear of death, let there be faith
Where there is desperation, let there be peace
Where there is sin, let there be grace
Where there is half-heartedness,
    let there be fervor
Where there is selfishness, let there be giving
Where there is calculation, let there be generosity
Where there is atheism, let there be adoration
Where there is darkness, let there be light
Where there is lewdness, let there be virginity
Where there is self-abasement, let there be
    strength of character
Where a child rebels, let there be submission
Where the father is unworthy, let there be
    your discipline
Where there is sadness, let there be joy

Where there is emptiness, let it be filled
Where there is death, let there be life
Where there is exploitation, let there be
   correctness
Where there is theft, let there be giving
Where there is arrogance, let there be humility
Where there is power, let there be caring
Where there is communism, let there be
   the spirit of community
Where there is racism, let there be catholicism
Your kingdom come.

(*The Desert Journal*, p. 34)

Real poverty is feeling yourself to be nothing because you possess nothing. It is a poverty in spirit which has no more pretensions, which no longer relies on itself because it has nothing, which counts for nothing. I would say that it is the shape of humility, the outward garment of humility.

I have always trusted in the Father's providence, and I have always experienced poverty as detachment from the goods of earth. But . . . what pride I had in my internal treasures, my ideas, my scheme! They were my riches. I was rich. I felt myself to be so rich that I could even give to the Church, give to my brothers and sisters, save them, save them.

What a wretch I was! This was sin! What could I give my brothers and sisters? Words, empty words!

(Letters to Dolcidia, p. 60)

Those Who Live by the Sword Will Die by the Sword

"It seems right that laws make humane provisions for the case of those who for reasons of conscience refuse to bear arms" (*Gaudium et Spes*, 79).

We should lose nothing by forming young conscientious objectors into "peace corps" to reconstruct villages destroyed in earthquakes, give schooling to illiterate people, bring assistance to lepers or the starving. In peace-time there is no problem. But in war? It is better to say nothing here for fear of infuriating the "moderates," the defenders of established order, nationalist fanatics. But one tiny plea I shall make. Members of government, think twice before declaring war. That is all I ask: think twice!

It could be that *not* declaring war is the better solution. Take extreme care. You might give bayonets to youngsters who use them to cut flowers to welcome the arriving enemy: "please come in, won't you? there's coffee ready."

You will no doubt call me a defeatist.

I suppose it is a question of deciding whether the young Austrian who preferred to be condemned to death by a military tribunal rather than take up arms with Hitler was a martyr or a traitor.

It is a question of deciding whether a few voices raised against Mussolini in protest to his invasion of Ethiopia were more Christian than the screams of the masses intoxicated by an undiscriminating nationalism and blinded by colossal historical ignorance.

It is a question of deciding whether those who in Algeria refused to obey orders to torture prisoners in the service of victory at any price were defeatists or Christians.

In short, it is a question of deciding whether someone has the right to trample on my conscience merely because he is in charge, whether the State can force me to take part in its schemes . . . when they are evil.

Perhaps as never before the moment has come in which we shall see blossoming in a soil plowed by the atrocious suffering of thousands of wars the flower of humanity's conscience able to stand firm not only in defense of belief in Christ, as in times past, but — and this would be new — in defense of belief in the human person.

(*Love is for Living*, p. 142-144)

New Heaven and New Earth

"Then I saw a new heaven and a new earth; for the first heaven and the first earth had passed away, and the sea was no more. And I saw the holy city, new Jerusalem, coming down out of heaven . . ." (Rv 21:1).

The new heaven and the new earth promised by the Spirit, which constitute the substance of our faith, will be truly new and not old things restored. God does not expect anything from us in order to remake, recreate the heaven and the earth. God's work absolutely does not depend on the stage we have reached. What could he expect from us, anyway?

"When the Son of man comes, will he find faith on earth?" (Lk 18:8).

What could he expect from us when we may already be on the brink of destroying the world with our atomic explosions?

I make a new heaven and a new earth, says Christ in Revelations. In other words: I am making another creation because things that existed are no longer. Our entire faith consists in believing in the divine possibility.

What will be left from our earthly city?

Only love will survive.

Our home will disappear, but the affection that linked us will survive. Our office will disappear, but our daily toil to earn our bread will survive. All human revolutions will disappear, but the tears shed for justice will survive. Our worn bodies will disappear, but the wounds of our sacrifice and struggle will survive. However, they will survive on a body which has been recreated, which is transparent, divine, the offspring of the resurrection, and no longer slave of our former death. In fact, the first token of this hope is given to us by Christ's resurrection.

(Ogni Giorno un Pensiero, p. 18)

The kingdom of heaven means God with us.

No piece of news could be more elating.

God is my ally. My life becomes divine life, my life's story, sacred history.

The kingdom of heaven means God with us.

The messianic times are times in which this truth is announced and made possible through the will of God.

It is the summary of the gospels, the good news to the poor.

And who are the poor?

I am the poor; I'm a child of God crying out its limitations and inability from the bosom of a dark generation.

Now this is being announced to me and I become aware of it.

It is announced to me today.

The truth had always been there but it did not mean much to me because I was not mature enough to receive it.

God means little to me unless I discover that God is alive.

There is no point in God's coming to me if I do not see him.

The messianic time is the time of love, that is, the time in which I become aware of God's *other*.

The preceding times have prepared the coming, the messianic time *is* the coming.

Now is the time of love.

Now is the time of communication.

It is life shared by two.

It is the beginning of my life of holiness.

My life of holiness begins as soon as I experience, through faith, that from now on I shall no longer walk on my own, but with God.

Thus, my fears are gone.

(*Ogni Giorno un Pensiero*, p. 193)

This Is My Body,
This Is My Blood

The eucharist is central to our Christian faith and it was thus that Little Brother Carlo wrote a great deal about the eucharist.

The eucharist is so ordinary one could even say so mundane; bread and wine, simple gifts offered to God in thanksgiving and returned to us as the body and blood of Christ.

We hear a mother say to her child, "I want to eat you all up." In this expression we hear love and affection. This is a rather primitive realization that when we love there is a magnificent unity between persons. There is a desire to share one with another. It seems to me we eat to live but we also love in order to live. It is in our experience of Eucharist that we both live and share in a communion with another, with the Christian community and with our God. The eucharist becomes for us a way to share in love. When we celebrate the eucharist we actively participate in the work of God which is the work of love.

Vatican II reminds us that the eucharist is central to all of our worship. It is in the eucharist that we find our meaning and we bind together as a community.

When I reflect upon our lives I ask the question, "Are we any different from the bread and wine we offer?" It seems to me we are no different, we are just as ordinary. Yet by God's spirit we are God touched and share in the divine life offered to us in Jesus the Christ. It seems to me that like the bread and wine offered in thanksgiving become the Body and Blood of Christ so too do we, touched by the divine Spirit, become the Body of Christ.

I Am the Bread of Life!

You will tell me I am old-fashioned to go on believing in visits to the Blessed Sacrament. Still, I do believe Jesus is present in the eucharist not only during the mass, but also between one mass and the next: always. And how helpful this belief has been to me; what great things this presence has given me!

It was here, before it, that I learned to pray

When, in the desert, my novice master left me alone for eight days; when, later on, I remained alone in a hermitage for forty days, I would have gone mad had it not been for this presence answering to the needs of my presence, this love responding to the demands of my love.

It is here that I have felt the presence of God most strongly; it is here that I have experienced for myself Christ's dramatic recapitulation of the history of salvation

And, always come back here when I want to make my way to the threshold of the invisible, because the eucharist is the surest doorway opening on to it.

(*In Search of the Beyond*, p. 111)

I could pray outside under the stars, which represent the cosmos for me; I could pray with the

Bible, which is the Word of God but, if I can, I prefer to pray before the eucharist, which is the very presence of him for whom everything was created and who was revealed by the Bible as Savior of the world.

The eucharist recapitulates the cosmos for me; the eucharist recapitulates the Bible for me. All three bear divine within them, and all three are worthy to be there while I am praying, but the third is the greatest.

The eucharist is the fullness of the gift, it is the pearl hidden in the mystery of Scripture, the treasure in the field of the Word of God, the secret of the king. In the eucharist God becomes a presence beside me on my path, bread in my knapsack, friendship close to my heart as another person. To those who have not the courage to say there is nothing there and leave the tabernacle unattended; to those who behave as though there were no living presence there, I would say: assume that it is true; assume that under the sacramental sign there is the living presence of Jesus. Assume that faith, it is the authentic response to such a sublime reality; surely I am justified in coming to spend a bit more time here in his presence.

You will say: but the eucharist was made to be eaten, Jesus said so himself. That is true, and I shall eat it tomorrow, and the day after tomorrow, and so on to the last day of my life; but between

one meal and another, one agape and another, is
Jesus absent from me? Has he given me his body
and withheld himself? Has he given me his blood
and denied me his friendship?

I need bread, but I assure you I feel the need of
friendship quite as much, and nothing gives me
the friendship of Jesus more than the gospel and
the eucharist.

(In Search of the Beyond, p. 110)

This bread speaks to me of humility, of lowli-
ness, of self-giving. It tells me of the parable he
invented to explain to me and to explain himself,
it epitomizes for me his preferences, which find in
the bread the model and symbol dearest to him.
Bread, not stone; bread, not luxuries; bread, not
arms; bread, not punishment; bread, not gold.

Above all, it tells me that it is with this bread —
with which he became bread — that he will nourish me for eternal life, "Anyone who eats this
bread will live forever" (Jn 6:58).

(In Search of the Beyond, p. 112)

You Are the Body of Christ!

What does Jesus do in the eucharist? I have thought about it often. In the eucharist Jesus is immobilized not in one leg only, but both, and in his hands as well. He is reduced to a little piece of white bread. The world needs him so much and he doesn't move!

The eucharist is the silence of God, the weakness of God.

To reduce himself to bread while the world is so noisy, so agitated, so confused.

It is as though the world and the eucharist were walking in opposite directions. And they seem to get further and further from one another.

One has to be courageous not to let oneself be carried along by the world's march; one needs faith and willpower to go cross-current toward the eucharist, to stop, to be silent, to worship. And one needs really strong faith to understand the impotence and defeat which the eucharist represents and which is today what the impotence and defeat of Calvary was yesterday.

(*Letters from the Desert*, p. 130)

Become What You Eat!

But also to have Jesus in the host, hidden in the hut; to adore him, pray to him, love him, and obtain from him the strength not to rebel, not to curse, but to accept lovingly what the day would bring.

(Letters from the Desert, p. 120)

It was near to Christmas.

I wanted to prepare for Christmas in solitude, and the place I had chosen was Ouarourout where water was abundant and a small natural cave could serve as a chapel.

But the weather soon changed and the desert became cold and grey due to the high mist that covered the sun.

I was in a cave with a shepherd, Ali.

I was cold.

There were sheep and the stench of dung.

Nothing was missing.

The eucharist that I had hung round my neck made me think of Jesus present there under the sign of bread.

The night advanced. Outside the storm continued to rage over the desert.

Now all was silence in the cave.

The sheep filled up the available space.

Ali slept curled in his cloak with his head resting on the back of a sheep and with two lambs at his feet.

Meanwhile I prayed, reciting Luke's gospel from memory: "And while they were there, the time came for her to be delivered. And she gave birth to her first-born son and wrapped him in swaddling clothes, and laid him in a manger, because there was no place for them in the inn" (Lk 2:26). Then I was silent and waited.

Mary became my prayer and I felt her to be very, very close to me.

Jesus was in the eucharist just there under my cloak.

All my faith, all my hope, all my love were united in one point.

(*Blessed Are You Who Believed*, pp. 14-16)

Bread is food.

The eucharist is food.

Before being friendship, God is bread. Before being your judge he is your food. In fact he has said: "I did not come to condemn the world but to save it" (Jn 12:47).

He is not the boss watching me, he is the brother who feeds me.

And he is the food that transforms me.

(*The God Who Comes*, p. 119)

May Your Spirit Transform this Bread and Wine into the Body and Blood of Christ!

The eucharist is dead without prayer, just as faith is dead without works.

Love by yourself remains sterile and empty: it has no reply to welcome and to fertilize it.

We cannot listen to God's "yes" without offering him our "yes."

God's "yes" is the sacrament of the eucharist; our "yes" is prayer.

Here, I think, is the real reason for the frequent unfruitfulness and sterility of the sacraments; they are just performed as rites, to which one can no longer reply with living, personal prayer.

The eucharist given to someone who does not pray is like food given to a corpse; it increases the smell.

(*The God Who Comes*, p. 126)

He became transformed into a piece of bread.

> . . . the Lord Jesus on the night in which he was betrayed took bread, and after he had given thanks, broke it and said, "This is my body, which is for you. Do this in remembrance of me." In the same way, after the supper, he took

the cup, saying, "This cup is the new covenant of my blood. Do this, whenever you drink it, in remembrance of me" (1 Cor 11:23-25).

It is difficult to believe Christ's words, which are so tremendous and amazing.

But it is equally difficult to get away from them.

I cannot avoid them any longer, and if I did, I should be sinning against the Spirit.

That is why I say, "I believe in what Jesus said; I believe that this bread of life is Christ near me, Christ become bread for me, and Christ become presence in me."

I know that this act of faith is dark as the night, but nothing is clearer than this night. I have gazed for days and days at this bread, I have lived for weeks in caves in the desert with this presence alone, and always, always he has said to me in faith, "It is I, do not be afraid. It is I, and I love you.

"Do not be afraid of the darkness, be a child before my words.

"I wanted to become bread to be eaten by men and women, because by eating me, they are feeding upon eternal life.

"Why do you find it strange that I should have wanted to become bread through love?

"Have you had no experience of love?

"When you have loved, really loved, have you not wanted to become bread for your beloved?

"Oh, to be able to enter the body of the person you love!

"Would not a mother do this for her child?

"Does not the bridegroom do this for the bride?"

You can argue about the eucharist as much as you like, but on the day love really takes hold of you, perhaps you will understand that Jesus is not a fool or madman.

To be able to become bread!

To be able to nourish the whole world with his flesh and blood!

(*The God Who Comes*, p. 114)

Broken and Poured Out — Forsaken, So We Might Live!

If I could become bread to feed all the poor, I should throw myself into the fire at once. No, the eucharist is not something strange: It is the most logical thing in the world, it is the story of the greatest lover ever lived in this world, by a man called Jesus.

When I gaze on this bread, when I take up this bread into my hands, I gaze on and take up the passion and death of Christ for humanity. This bread is the memorial of his death for us. This bread is the trumpet call of the resurrection, through which we, too, shall one day be able to rise.

This bread is the living summary of all God's love for humanity.

From Genesis to the prophets, from Exodus to the Apocalypse, everything is yearning toward this terrible mystery of God's tragic love for humanity. God, who made himself present in the first covenant and yet more present in the Incarnation, becomes still more present in this mystery of the bread of life.

You can hold God in your hand as a piece of bread, it is a close, personal presence.

(*The God Who Comes*, p. 116)

One of the commonest difficulties in the spiritual life of men and women today is this very crossing from hubbub into silence, from childishness into maturity of faith, from a surplus of statues to the starkness of the eucharist, from preoccupation with self to charity, from sentimentality to aridity, from impressive processions to the poverty-ridden streets of the human city.

Faced with the harsh realities of demythologization and secularization, many Christians — too many — are positively terrified.

(*Summoned by Love*, p. 58)

I Am with You Always

It seems to me that there is no place that we could ever be that would be outside of God or away from God. There is nothing we could do that would separate us from the love God has for us. God is here among us, in our midst. It is said that God is closer to us than we are to ourselves. In fact there is no way to escape God. Psalm 139 reminds us that there is nowhere that one can go to escape God, neither the highest mountain nor the deepest ocean. No, God is ever present at all times and in all places.

It seems that it is best to say that we walk about in a cloud of our own making. We walk with a self-imposed blindness. We walk around with our eyes closed stating that there is no God and yet all we need do is open our eyes and see in whose midst we live, move and have our being.

Like the very breath that fills our lungs and the air that we live immersed in so it is with God. God is everywhere sustaining us yet if we choose to hold our breath we might claim that we can't breathe or that we do not need air but life's journey shows us that we need the air around us, we cannot live without the air. So too, it is with our experience of God. God is everywhere and at all times loving us into being. God is here even now. Whether we want God to be here or not there is no way to escape the love that fashioned the sun, the moon and the stars.

It Is the Spirit That Will Teach Us How to Pray!

And he will lead you higher still if you put into operation a system which I have discovered only recently: "Walk standing still." That is, be terribly active and at the same time totally passive. Incline your will, but keep very still before God. Don't move. Don't even move your lips, listen in silence. It's up to him to speak, it's up to him "to carry you." It's not easy, I can assure you, because silence frightens us and stillness seems like a waste of time to us. And yet the mystical life is silence and stillness "in him."

(*Letters to Dolcidia,* p. 88)

But let us begin at the beginning. Learning to pray means, above all, identifying oneself with every aspect of earthly existence. Anyone who prays to God must be, or endeavor to become, one who looks on the whole of creation with a sympathetic eye — on all reality, physical and spiritual; on nature and on grace; on the rocks on which we place our feet, and on the angels in whom we believe on the testimony of Christ and who inhabit the invisible world. As long as we are unable to accept creation, we will be unable to enter into a relationship of love with the God who fashioned

and sustains it, and who continues to fashion and
sustain what he has created.

(In Search of the Beyond, p. 98)

But through the grace of God, contemplation —
true contemplation — does not depend on you.
You are not the dawn, you are the land that awaits
the dawn.

Your God is the dawn, and later he is full day-
light, and later still high noon.

You are the land that waits for the light, the
blackboard that waits for the white chalk of the
draftsman who walks toward you with that chalk
in his hand. Sit down and try to be still; sit still and
try to hope. Leave behind you time, space, number, thought, reason, culture and look ahead.

(In Search of the Beyond, p. 90)

And God Has Smiled on Us!

At this point let us call to mind one very important thing: prayer is not so much a matter of
talking as listening; contemplation is not watching but being watched.

On the day when we realize this, we will have
entered finally into possession of the truth, and
prayer will have become a living reality. To be
watched by God: that is how I would define contemplation, which is passive rather than active,
more a matter of silence than words, of waiting
rather than action.

(*In Search of the Beyond*, p. 86)

The path of prayer is as long as a person's life,
neither more nor less. It is now a glorious path
through the meadows, now a peaceful country
road with no obstacles where we can abandon
ourselves to quiet thought, now a rough mule-
track winding up the mountains, now a way over
the bare rocks on the summit. Sometimes it is like
a city street full of noise and distraction, at others
it follows the water off the streets into under-
ground drains and so to the river or sea, carrying
with it the rubbish and filth of life.

But it is always prayer.

It is still prayer, I believe, even when it is silence and looks to the observer like a dried-up bed of a stream. Surely a blade of grass bent with the heat is still a prayer in heaven's eyes even though it cannot ask for water.

Surely the pitiable state of those reduced to running sores by loneliness and evil is a prayer, even though they say nothing but speak with their lives.

(*Love is for Living*, p. 126)

My life is worth living if I can learn to ransom everything that happens to me into love, in imitation of Jesus: because *love is for living*.

When I meet brothers or sisters of mine who have caused me great pain in the past by viciously calumniating me, I shall love them and in loving them I shall transform the evil done to me into good: because *love is for living*.

When I have to live with people who do not see things the way I see them, who say they are enemies of my faith, I shall love them, and in loving them I shall sow the seeds of the future dialogue in my heart and theirs: because *love is for living*.

When I go into a shop to by something for myself — clothes, food, or whatever it may be — I shall think of my brothers and sisters who are poorer than I am, of the hungry and the naked, and I shall use this thought to govern my purchase, trying out of love to be tight with myself and generous with them: because *love is for living*.

When I see time's destructive traces in my body and the approach of old age, I shall try to love even more in order to transform the coldest season of life into a total gift of myself in preparation for the imminent holocaust: because *love is for living*.

When I see the evening of my life, or, on the tarmac in a car accident, in the agony of a fatal illness, in the ward of a geriatric hospital, feel the end coming, I shall reach out again for love, striving to accept in joy whatever fate God has had in store for me: because *love is for living*.

Yes, love is God in me, and if I am in love I am in God, that is, in life, in grace: a sharer in God's being.

(Love is for Living, p. 135)

God Took Me By the Hand!

It all started that day on which, in a strip of the desert, in the solitude of Sahara, I dreamed of being smashed by a large granite rock under which I had fallen asleep while taking a rest.

In my dream, I was led before God's judgment and was judged on love; nothing else but love.

Because of my refusal to give a blanket to a poor person, I was promptly dispatched to purgatory, where I understood that in order to get out of it I was supposed to carry out a perfect act of love; that is, an act of the same nature of Jesus' love.

I felt I wasn't up to it.

Many years have gone by since then and precisely yesterday, Good Friday, while meditating once more on the passion of Jesus, I realized I had not made any progress since that day under the large rock.

I know now that I am unable to love perfectly. I do not have the strength to follow Jesus to Calvary.

On the other hand, is it possible ever to feel capable?

And if I did feel capable and strong, would I not be even worse than what I actually am?

This is the truth I have finally discovered in the arduous journey of my religious experience.

If it depended solely on me then I would never be truly capable!

An event must take place, a passage crossed; lightning must flash, someone must arrive, something must happen in order for us . . . to become capable.

Still, I shall never be able to discover it, to anticipate it, to foresee it!

I must only wait in prayer, loving, crying, begging.

That is the attitude we are supposed to assume on earth.

God, who is the God of the impossible, will appear unexpectedly and by touching my soul will make me capable of following him to the place he has established for me, as it happened to the thief on that Good Friday afternoon.

(*Ogni Giorno un Pensiero*, p. 87)

I don't know how it happened to you, but I know how it happened to me. God arrived in my heart like a huge parable. Everything around me spoke of him.

The sky spoke to me of him,

the earth spoke to me of him,

the sea spoke to me of him.

He was like a secret hidden in all things, visible and invisible.

He was like the solution to all problems.

He was like the most important person who had ever entered my life and with whom I should have lived for ever.

Very soon I felt myself enveloped by him as a "presence always present," one who looked at me from all the leaves of the wood I was walking through, and across the clouds riding briskly along the sky above my head.

I have never had any difficulty in feeling God's presence, especially when I was small.

Rather, his absence would have seemed very strange and very unlikely.

I felt myself to be in God
like a bird in the air
like a log in the fire
like a baby in its mother's womb.

This last image was the strongest, the truest, and it is always growing.

I truly think that a woman's womb containing a baby is the theme of the whole universe, the visibility of invisible things, the sign of the way God works in order to make me his son.

(*The Desert in the City*, p. 25)

And this evening I, too, want to come to you brother or sister.

Do you know why?

To bear witness to you in the Holy Spirit that God is the living God.

Because this is the task of the Christian community: to bear witness to our belief to each other.

And I bear witness to it before you: I believe!

You do not see God in things and he is in things.

You do not see God in history and he is in history.

You do not see God in your room and he is in your room.

He is there where you are at this minute.

And he is looking at you and wants to communicate with you from the depths of his being.

(*The Desert in the City*, p. 90)

Waiting

If I were asked what the most important thing is for us who wish to believe in a Christianity that has an actual bearing upon our modern life, I would say it is the defeat of fear. In fact, I don't pray because I am afraid of wasting time and feeling spiritually dry. But all our heavenly spouse asks of us is to be faithful while we await his arrival.

He is the approaching God. Therefore, we must be prepared for the encounter, being certain, however, that he will always bring us something new.

The freshness of the Church consists in believing in the novelty of God. Doesn't today's Church suffer, perchance, the temptation of fear?

God is a novelty. And when I see a Church that fears novelty, I cannot but smile. The Church's remaining on its feet does not depend on our personal behavior. The Church stands on its feet because it has the Spirit.

The attitude of those who wish to make room for contemplation in their lives is precisely this certainty of God. It is this testimony that makes our faith cry out: "The risen Christ is our strength!" And that is why, particularly today, we must convey the impression in our Church that we do not need other certainties. It is precisely in this courage, in not seeking any guarantees and in putting my faith not on an organization, not — should I say — on my former prayers, but in abandoning myself confidently to the power of the risen Christ, to the action of the Holy Spirit who lives in me and to the infinite confidence in a Father who sustains my life, that I find my peace and, therefore, my contemplation.

(*Ogni Giorno un Pensiero*, p. 19)

The Novelty

Whenever I pray and he makes me wait in his absence, whenever I search his presence and he shows me his darkness and I resist, do you know what comes to mind? God's novelty. On this earth, by now everything bores me except God's novelty. God is always new, God is the eternal novelty.

At first God seems to be absent from our prayer and we remain in darkness and aridity throughout the night. We search him like the spouse in the Canticle and smell his perfume, which has impregnated our clothing. However, once we overcome the passage, which is the mystery of Christ and is called Easter, death, then we are born to true contemplation.

In his youth, Saint Francis would sing on the Subasio: "Praised be my Lord for Brother Fire."

His song was full of poetry, feeling, youth. Yet, while in the grotto of Sassospigola at Verna, with his eyelids closed from illness and his heart broken by the suffering caused by a congregation that did not wish to follow him in his suffering, by the refusal of his own monks to understand him, precisely in that moment, when reduced to passivity, Francis was struck by the cherubim. Whether or not the stigma constitute an actual fact is not important, since they are only signs. In fact, what really counts is Francis' readiness to the action God wishes to fulfill upon his perfect passivity.

When in our prayer to the Father we are able to overcome the discomfort of the passage, then a new reality actually starts, we live the life of Christ. Each of us is called to follow Jesus in his footsteps. And our greatness on this earth is precisely the fact that we are called to live the same life of Jesus. And at the center of Jesus's life is Easter, which we sing to and bears a single message: that life stems from death. Even contemplation, which is life, is born from death. It is death of having to wait, the death of our spiritual dryness through which God leads us to the fulfillment of Jesus' prayer: "Father . . . not my will but yours be done" (Lk 22:42).

(*Ogni Giorno un Pensiero*, p. 36)

A continuous acceptance of the presence of God in all that surrounds us is only a start. It is still necessary to take another step based on our faith.

This second step consists in discovering the person of God. Every time we let ourselves be kissed by the sun, every time we touch the earth and sing together with Saint Francis, "Praised be my Lord . . . Praised be my Lord for Brother Fire," we are still at the threshold of contemplation. At that point, our fresh and beautiful heart expresses itself, but we have still not reached true contemplation. Contemplation is a passive stage, and in order to reach it you must discover the person.

When Abraham was in the desert and heard God's voice saying: "Leave your country . . . offer me your son!" his general faith in God present throughout the desert became a faith in the God-person standing before him. When Moses saw the bramble-bush burning he didn't turn right or left but looked straight ahead.

It is the personalization of God. The discovery of this person coincides with the mystery of our own individuality. I, as an individual, feel the presences of the other person before me. Thus, life is expressed in one word: Father. Light becomes one word: Jesus. Love becomes a person: Holy Spirit.

Still, there is more to it than that. In fact, we would suffer if they remained like that, as if unity was broken between the three. However, through the revelation of the Holy Spirit who is love, we regain the sense of God's unity.

Then we relive the experience of Abraham, who despite seeing three men before him, cries "My Lord God" in the singular (cf. Gn 18:3).

This discovery of God's unity through the trinity of the persons is the substance of contemplation and when it becomes a personal matter, we experience a joy not comparable to any earthly joy; that is the kingdom itself.

(Ogni Giorno un Pensiero, p. 111)

Everything Is Prayer

If a priest pauses to pray after an entire day's work, I would ask him what he has done so far. Everything is prayer.

In fact, if we manage to compose this kind of unity, everything we do becomes prayer.

Then the eight hours you spend working as a nurse at a patient's bedside or as a clerk behind a desk can be performed with the same intensity, the same intimacy, as when you kneel and think — this time perhaps more strongly —about your God. But, if you still feel there is a contrast between your work and your prayer, it means you have not yet reached the stage of contemplation. In fact, it is not required of us to be kneeling to receive God's revelation. God can reveal himself to us while were are driving our car, or while we are at rest or while we are playing. As John the Apostle says (cf. Jn 14:21-23), the revelation consists in Christ's promise in the matter of love.

If you love me do what I have told you to, I shall reveal myself to you.

If you do what I have told you to, my Father will love you, we will come to you and make our dwelling place with you.

(*Ogni Giorno un Pensiero*, p. 117)

I can no longer look at a flower, a hill, or a meadow without thinking of God. Nor can I spend, in fact, three minutes without thinking of God. Yet, thinking is too small a word to describe it.

It is rather something deeper and it depends on contemplation, which is a gift from God. If I were to tell you what the experience of being in God feels like, I would say it feels like being a fish in the water, a bird in the sky or, even better a child in its mother's womb.

The image of a child in its mother's womb is the most perfect image of God's action on us. We are in God, we breathe in God and we live in God.

However, it is not an impersonal experience.

God touches us personally. God touches us with the sun, with the wind, with history, with suffering and with the events unfolding around us.

God's action is constant generation.

Yet, many find it difficult to believe in God because they feel him distant from their lives. If only they knew how close God is to us, what the vital reality uniting us to God is, they would be amazed at learning how wrong they were.

God is either everything or nothing.

If God exists, as he does, if God is a father who sustains me and generates me to the light, to love, then I am always within him and there is no need to search unity with him. That unity is already present. It is reality. We must only become conscious of it. Contemplation consists in becoming aware of this absolute presence of God in our lives.

(*Ogni Giorno un Pensiero*, p. 139)

Like God

If we are not capable during our lifetime of falling in love with God, we are lost.

Without love we are incomplete, immature, bored, missing paradise.

We would be doubtful and formulate the following equation: love of God equals peace, joy, bliss, fecundity, exultation, paradise; lack of love equals war, sadness, loneliness, sterility, death, hell . . .

"You, therefore, must be perfect, as your heavenly Father is perfect" (Mt 5:48).

The requirements of the kingdom are the same requirements of love, which, by its very nature, sees us or makes us all equal.

The love of God compels us to become like God, similar to God, with the just that follow God.

There is no way out.

Since God loves the light, we too should love the light.

Since God forgives, we too must forgive

Since God dies for love, we too should be ready to die for love.

To build the kingdom means precisely to work and act to become similar to God, following Christ as a model.

The kingdom is not built by our chatting, but rather by our acting.

The kingdom advances every time we carry out a concrete deed in response to love, which is God.

Every time I feed the hungry,

Every time I visit the imprisoned,

Every time I clothe the naked,

Every time I forgive the enemy,

Every time I share my belongings,

Every time I console the afflicted,

Every time I pray for the living and the dead.

Moreover, since love calls for equality, we shall love God with the same power of God's love for us.

Which is, in one word, paradise.

(*Ogni Giorno un Pensiero*, p. 270)

I Am the Resurrection

"Behold I make all things new." In the resurrection of Jesus we see the transformation of all things. Jesus is the first fruit of all those who have died. We as Christians believe in the total transformation of all creation. Already all creation is charged with the grandeur of God, yet still we await God's fullness to be revealed.

It seems that all the earth groans, waiting for the fullness of God's revelation. We are earth made, but heaven bound. The power of the resurrection reminds us that we too in our own earthly existence will be transformed by God's Holy Spirit.

In God there is mercy in the sight of sin, there is healing amidst suffering and sickness, there is satisfaction for the starving, joy replaces sorrow and life, life eternal replaces death.

He Died So that We Might Live

The more we love, the less we shall have to suffer.

Have you ever wondered about the meaning of a candle and what it stands for?

The use of candles can be traced to the night of Passover, the Lord's Easter.

The early Christians used candles to symbolize Christ's presence amidst the darkness of the world.

Just as Christ is the light of the world and has consummated himself for love, the candle offers its light by consummating itself.

It is a sign and, as every sign, it speaks to us.

The candle has revealed to me a lot. I fixed my eyes on it at great length on the night of Easter's Eve and made it mine on Sunday during mass.

Later I made greater progress in understanding the meaning of the flame consummating the wax.

Once, while I was in Vienna, a friend of mine gave me one of those beautiful colored candles as a gift. I took it home and placed it close to a small icon, on a chest of drawers I had in my cell.

It was like building a small altar.

Since then, whenever I experience suffering, which happens often and makes me feel as if I were inside a black hole, I light the candle. Then

I watch it closely and try to repeat to myself the words I so easily say to my brothers during the liturgy of light.

"Do you see this candle? It symbolizes Jesus giving his light to the world, and it is burning just as Jesus consummated himself."

After saying these words I try to pluck up courage and carry on my own personal simple liturgy, by doing three small things that come to mind and which I carry out in the right order:

I pray,

I love,

I wait.

(*Ogni Giorno un Pensiero*, p. 130)

I Will Be with You Always!

If only we could stay calm in our tribulations!

This victory, this peace, is not easily attained and we are given an entire life to reach it. Ours is a strong commitment, it consists in building, brick by brick, the edifice of our religiosity, in opening ourselves gradually to the gift of faith, which depends only on God, through continuous "acts of faith" that depend on us and our commitment. In this, like in everything else, God wants our cooperation. God's future gifts depend on our present commitment just as the athlete's strength depends on his training.

David's faith was stronger after accepting Goliath's challenge, just as Joshua's union with God increased after attacking Jericho without valid weapons. Judith was dearer to God after accepting through her faith to enter Holofernes' tent, just as Joseph became more "just" after saying "yes" to the angel who advised him to take Mary as his spouse.

Every act of faith we make trains us to trust God. Thus, our trust becomes every day stronger and leads us to the most absolute intimacy and the most perfect unity with God.

(*Ogni Giorno un Pensiero*, p. 166)

Since I discovered God as a person with whom I can speak, I have started to ask God questions. It is only fair that a child speaks to its father.

However, I asked you for bread and you gave me unemployment. I asked you for fish and you gave me the serpent of disease. I asked you for an egg and you gave me the scorpion of death. Why did Jesus have to cross my path? Why?

Perhaps to make me understand that that which resembles a stone is actually bread, that the lack of bread itself is bread. It was necessary for me to suffer in order to understand. Christ has taught me that my sickness was not really a serpent and that nothing can fulfill me more than suffering. Jesus taught me this to help me quiet down and return, as an individual, to the nature of contemplation, to make peace with my Father. Understanding this was necessary for me. This is God's revelation.

Christ is the revelation of the Father. Christ sees things as they actually are, and does not ask to change them. After him, children have continued to die; people have continued to die. Christ has not changed anything, he has only accepted. He has not asked the Father to change them.

Carrying upon himself the sign of Jonah, Christ plunges into the sea of the will of God and accepts death. And it is precisely there, at the bottom of his death, that the Father raises him to life.

Christ's prophecy is summarized by these words: "Life stems from death." Indeed, life stems from death. I do not have the power to change anything. I must accept things as they are to become free. I must accept now that which appears to me as a stone to understand eventually that it was, in fact, wholesome bread.

(*Ogni Giorno un Pensiero*, p. 222)

The Poor You Will Have with You Always!

As long as there is one hungry person on earth, you are there.

As long as there is one person suffering on earth, you are there.

As long as there is one person to be set free, you are there.

And if I want to be with you, I have to be with people.

There is no way round this.

I cannot deceive myself about this.

And anyhow, I should not want to do so, once having understood this.

And I feel solidarity with these new-wave Christians who have understood this.

Beside my mourning brother or sister, let me mourn.

Beside the prisoner, let me stay in prison.

I cannot accept resurrection, unless I first accept death.

The Easter mystery is not only about the resurrection, is not only the joy of Easter Sunday.

Primarily it is about the painful solidarity of Good Friday.

How unworthy of love — true love, I mean — to want to rejoice alone with Christ!

How unfair to crowd into his banquet, yet leave him alone to his sorrow and revulsion in the Garden of Olives!

It is so unfair that, in our more lucid moments, we should rather not accept paradise, without first — weak as we are — sharing something of his passion.

Who could resist him — Man of sorrows?

Who that loves him, that is?

This is why the delights of this world, of "this house of pleasures" as the pagans conceive it, repel me.

It is like feasting over a corpse.

Life regarded solely as pleasure, is not life; it is a brothel.

It is not worthy of Love.

I do not want it.

(*Summoned by Love*, pp. 91-92)

You Shepherd Us
Even in the Valley of Death

There is a reason for everything.

Love's first attitude toward the creation is to accept the creation, even if it seems strange, incomplete and sometimes hostile, to me.

There is a reason for everything.

Even Job's sufferings have a reason.

Even my polio stricken son has a reason.

Even David's sin has a reason.

Even the destruction of Jerusalem has a reason.

But before trying to free myself from the suffering that has befallen me, before taking my son to the hospital, before making any effective move to correct the evil surrounding me, I have to bow my head before the mystery, I have to put myself in the same attitude as Christ and take his words as mine, "Lord, let your will be done, not mine" (Lk 22:42).

(Summoned by Love, p. 94)

Yes, loving the negative in people.

Loving it in the certainty that tomorrow the positive will prevail.

Seen like this, the world no longer frightens me.

Seeing the city like this, I feel a hearty desire to act and to hope.

Before I understood these things, sin filled me with repulsion;

I thought of it as an enemy.

By the same token, I felt friendly toward the police who arrested prostitutes, and willingly preached on the perils of hell-fire to frighten the lads — to put the fear of God in them.

But now the sinner fills me with compassion; if I run into a prostitute I offer her a coffee; I have more hope in salvation, and the compassion which I feel for the sufferings of humankind is so intense that I utter the word "hell" far less often.

You might say — and this gives me intense and heart-felt joy — that I feel myself a friend to all, I am no longer upset when I meet someone who doesn't believe in God, I am more surprised when the opposite occurs; I cannot not belong to a sinful Church.

When I run into some "right-minded" person of the old moralizing type, I realize how the Church's slow progress is due to lack of confidence in the coming generations, and to the assumption that the old days exemplified the only way in which things should be done.

Yes, loving the negative in people, loving what is not yet in them.

(*Summoned by Love*, p. 100)

You Will Be with Me
this Day in Paradise

And what do the dying say to him?

People locked up in madhouses, human vegetables in chronic wards, the skeletal bodies of the aged, the misshapen, the children with Down's syndrome, the dwellers on the fringes of society, the cripples and the blind walking the streets of the world?

What do those people say to him who seek without finding, who have no hope, who have no faith, who couple alive and yet are dead?

I don't know.

Everyone tries to give an answer, but God for his part does not put the question. He says nothing.

And he says nothing, even when it is his beloved, his only son Jesus who is concerned.

"My God, my God, why have you forsaken me?" — and his cry is the concentrated cry of all mankind.

God says nothing.

And the sphere of clay goes on being kneaded by the fiery hand,

the living die,

the young grow old,

sunset goes on following sunrise,

heaven goes on reflecting earth
and the stars go on looking down on us as though nothing were happening.

Nothing stirs.

Far away in the silence, the agonized cry of Jesus echoes on:

"My God, my God, why have you forsaken me?"

I have already told you. — Don't try to understand, you won't succeed.

Don't try to see; you won't see.

Try to love.

In love and only in love can we be near Jesus forsaken and with him be near all the world's forsaken.

(Summoned by Love, pp. 114-115)

Jesus, Our Light in the Darkness

The ability to hope is the greatest gift that God would make to humanity.

When we are endowed with hope, we overcome the obstacles in which we are ensnared.

When we hope, we die already seeing our bodies in the resurrection light.

When we hope, we overcome fear, understand the purpose of ordeal, put our trust in God, believe in things which are impossible, feel God's presence in his darkness, begin to pray.

Abraham's hope is one of the wonders of humankind, and the hope of the martyrs is the radiance of the Church.

Hope is born when we experience the abyss of our helplessness, as Israel did in Babylon, as Jeremiah when lowered into the prison cistern, as Jesus on the cross.

And now I approach Jesus forsaken with greater understanding. In him, I see all the world's sufferings concentrated, the redemptive fire of humankind in evolution, the key to love's greatest secret.

In him, I have the answer to things which have no answer. In him, the soothing away of all my questions, the receptacle of all my neighbor's sufferings, the most sublime exemplar of Yahweh's poor man, the heroic mission of the true remnant of Israel, man made truly son of the Most High.

(*Summoned by Love*, pp. 116-117)

Do What She Tells You!

Mary, help me to believe.

Tell me what it means to believe in the resurrection of your son.

Listen, I am telling you, and remember what I say.
When you see a forest ravaged by storms,
and earthquakes blasting the land
and fire burning down your home
say to yourself: I believe
that the forest will come to life again
the land will be calm again
and I shall remake my home.

When you hear rumors of war and people everywhere are dying of terror, when "nation shall rise against nation and kingdom against kingdom" (Mt 24:7) say bravely to yourself, "Jesus warned me of this and he added: 'Look up and raise your heads, because your redemption is drawing near' " (Lk 21:28).

When sin has you in its grip and you feel utterly defeated, say to yourself, "Christ is risen from the dead and I shall rise from sin."

When old age or illness embitters your life, say "Christ is risen from the dead and has made a new heaven and a new earth." When you see your son running away from home in search of adventure and your cherished dream as father or mother crumbles around you, say "My son will not run away from God; he will come back because God loves him."

When charity seems to have vanished forever and you see men and women sunk in sin and drunk with treachery, say to yourself, "They will touch the depths but they will return because no one can live away from God."

When the world seems a defeat for God and you are sick with the disorder, the violence, the terror, the war on the streets; when the earth seems to be chaos, say to yourself, "Jesus died and rose again on purpose to save, and his salvation is already with us."

When your father or your mother, your son or your daughter, your spouse or your friend are on their deathbed, and you are looking at them in the pain of parting, say "We shall see each other again in the kingdom; courage."

This is what it means to believe in the resurrection.

But there is more.

Belief in the risen Christ means something else.

For Mother Teresa of Calcutta it means comforting the dying, and for you it means doing the same.

For Martin Luther King it meant facing death, and for you it means being unafraid to die for your brothers and sisters.

For Abbe' Shultz, prior of Taize', it means opening his convent to hope, and for you opening your house to hope.

Every departing missionary is an act of faith in the resurrection.

Every newly-opened leper hospital is an act of faith in the resurrection.

Every peace treaty is an act of faith in the resurrection.

Every agreed commitment is an act of faith in the resurrection.

When you forgive your enemy
When you feed the hungry
When you defend the weak
you believe in the resurrection.

When you have the courage to marry
When you welcome the newly-born child
When you build your home
you believe in the resurrection.

When you wake at peace in the morning
When you sing to the rising sun
When you go to work with joy
you believe in the resurrection.

Belief in the resurrection means filling life with faith,

it means believing in your brother or sister,

it means fearlessness toward all.

Belief in the resurrection means knowing that God is your father, Jesus your brother, and I, Mary, your sister and, if you like,

your Mother.

(*Blessed Are You Who Believed*, pp. 58-60)

Acknowledgments

In an anthology of readings it is sometimes difficult to locate all the copyright holders of the individual readings selected. If I have failed to acknowledge a copyright, please bring it to my attention, and a correction will take place. Thank you.

Carlo Carretto's writings cited in this book are being used with permission. I would like to thank the contributing publishers for their support in this anthology.

Blessed Are You Who Believed, translated by Barbara Wall, © 1982, Search Press (Kent: Burns & Oates, Ltd. 1982; Maryknoll: Orbis Books, 1983).

The Desert in the City, © Edizioni San Paolo (London: Harper Collins).

Love is for Living, translated by Jeremy Moiser, © 1976, Darton, Longman and Todd (Maryknoll: Orbis Books, 1985).

The Desert Journal, translated by Alison Swaisland Bucci, © 1992, HarperCollins Publishers (Maryknoll: Orbis Books, 1992).

The God Who Comes, translated by Rose Mary Hancock, © 1974, Orbis Books (London: Darton, Longman and Todd).

I Sought and I Found, translated by Robert R. Barr, © 1984 Orbis Books (London: Darton, Longman and Todd).

I, Francis, translated by Robert R. Barr, © 1982, Orbis Books (London: HarperCollins).

In Search of the Beyond, (London: Darton, Longman and Todd; Maryknoll: Orbis Books).

Letters from the Desert, translated by Rose Mary Hancock, © 1972, Orbis Books (London: Darton, Longman and Todd; Maryknoll: Orbis Books, 1972).

Letters to Dolcidia, translated by Michael J. Smith, © 1991, Harper-Collins Publishers (Maryknoll: Orbis Books, 1991).

Ogni Giorno un Pensiero, © 1993 Città Nuova (Rome: Città Nuova, 1993).

Summoned by Love, translated by Alan Neame, © 1977, Darton, Longman and Todd (Maryknoll: Orbis Books, 1978).

Also available from New City Press

SET YOUR HEARTS ON THE GREATEST GIFTS
Living the Art of Christian Love
by Morton Kelsey,

"A wise and compassionate book from Morton Kelsey, who distills a lifetime's learning and teaching about love in these pages. Poet, teacher, and psychologist, Kelsey uses his own rich experience to explain how we can grow in Christian love."
Spirit & Life

"This rich and full book is a cry of joy and hope to the church and to each one of us about what is the essence of the essence. Read it if you want to be reinspired by the core values of the Christian faith. Give it to anyone who wonders what Christianity is really about. Morton condenses a lifetime of wisdom and experience into this very readable compendium on love. Would that every Christian would read it. What a great selection for group study as well as personal reflection!"
Book Nook

"Kelsey writes movingly about his own slow learnings in the art of love during his son's battle with death. The best section of the book revolves around his own nighttime talks with God."
Values & Visions Magazine

ISBN 1-56548-043-0
paperback,-6 5 3/8 x 8 1/2, 216 pp., $12.95

To order phone 1- 800 - 462-5980

And . . .

THOMAS MERTON -- MY BROTHER
His Journey into Freedom, Compassion, and Final Integration
by M. Basil Pennington

"What I like in Pennington's book is also what I like most in Merton's work: clear and frequent admission of human frailty and foible, in combination with an intense longing for the life of prayer. Examining Merton within the Cistercian tradition, in context with Bernard of Clairvaux, in touch with Byzantine tradition, in terms of centering prayer and in many other dimensions, Pennington shows us a Merton of large spiritual vision—warts and all."

Review by Emilie Griffin
America

"An informed, sensitive and realistic look at Merton by a fellow-Cistercian. The book's value is enhanced by Fr. Pennington's extensive use of so-far unpublished Merton material — journals, recordings, mimeographed talks, etc."

Review by Frank Sadowski, SSP
Pastoral Life

"This book lifts up and celebrates Merton's great attentiveness and his gift for deep listening."

Review by Frederic A. Brussat
Values & Visions Magazine

ISBN 1-56548-039-2
paperback,-6 5 3/8 x 8 1/2, 208 pp., $12.95

To order phone 1- 800 - 462-5980